THE OGHAM

Sue Bagust

An introduction to the ancient alphabet of trees, their
uses and healing powers, and their meanings for
magic, divination and lunar astrology

THE OGHAM

CONTENTS

THE OGHAM

The Druid Peace Prayer

Deep within the centre of my being
　　　　　May I find peace

Silently within the centre of the grove
　　　　　May I share peace

Calmly within the circle of mankind
　　　　　May I be peace

May there be peace throughout the world

The Ogham
Beith-Luis-Nuin

Just as the romantic Victorians created a secret language of flowers to convey a message to those in the know, so the practical Celts developed a secret language of trees. Each tree has its own meaning, so a leaf from that tree carries a message to those who know the secret language. When a number of leaves are strung together they create a longer or more complex message like individual words create a sentence, and the leaves like words tell a story when they are read in sequence.

One of the more responsible tasks entrusted to an apprentice Druid was to replace the leaves when they became fragile from being handled. This could be why pages of our modern books are still known as leaves, where we get the saying *"turning over a new leaf"* and why we say *"leafing through"* a book meaning to scan the contents quickly.

THE OGHAM

The belief that trees have spirits of their own or are inhabited by spirits, especially any tree with a strong aura, is the base for the Ogham (pronounced Ohm).

The old Brehon Laws[1] revered trees and decreed that any person who deliberately harmed a tree should give his own life by giving his living intestines to bandage and heal the tree. The Celts also believed that trees could influence humans which probably gave our language the phrases *"touch wood"* and *"knock on wood"*.

Stands of trees multiplied the energy of the individual trees so groves became sacred places for meditation and for worship, linking the three worlds of Earth, Sea and Sky[2]. Faeries thrive where oak, ash and thorn grow together so this group of trees is still called the faery triad.

The Druids who were the priests or religious leaders of the ancient Celts had a kinship with trees revealed by this secret language which over time developed into being used as hand signals[3] and a written language instead of being sung, and then into a tree calendar and astrology as well as divination. When a message needed to be kept for longer than the life of a leaf, the secret alphabet could be carved onto a stone or marked on clay or on timber.

---

[1] Brehon Law is the body of ancient native Irish law set down on parchment in the 7th century and named after wandering lawyers, the Brehons. These laws were still followed in Gaelic areas until the English conquest of Ireland in the early 17th century.
[2] See Appendix 1: The Celtic World
[3] See Appendix 2: Etymology & Ogham variations

THE OGHAM

The original Ogham lists twenty feda[4] that represent trees of the northern hemisphere, divided into four families of five trees. These families of trees are called aicme, and each aicme is named after its first feda.

The Aicme Beith (the B Group)
    Beith (Birch)
    Luis (Rowan)
    Fearn (Alder)
    Saille (Willow)
    Nuin (Ash)

The Aicme Huatha (the H Group)
    Huatha (Hawthorn)
    Duir (Oak)
    Tinne (Holly)
    Coll (Hazel)
    Quert (Apple)

The Aicme Muin (the M Group)
    Muin (Vine)
    Gort (Ivy)
    Ngetal (Reed)
    Straif (Blackthorn)
    Ruis (Elder)

The Aicme Ailim (the A Group)
    Ailim (Pine or Silver Fir)
    Ohn (Furze)
    Ur (Heather)
    Eadha (Aspen or White Poplar)
    Ioho (Yew)

---

[4] Feda means tree, and Aicme translates to family.

THE OGHAM

The Ogham is one of the few languages written and read left to right and bottom to top and the Ogham symbols are straight lines which are easy to draw:

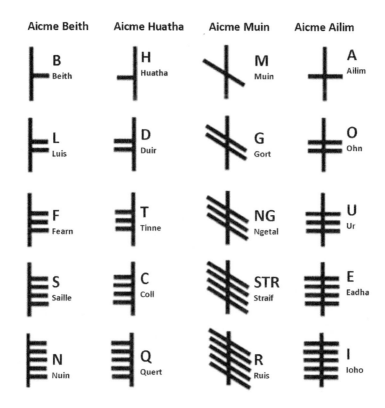

The Aicme Beith:
has lines drawn to the right of the edge-line so begin at the right side and use downward strokes

The Aicme Huatha:
has lines drawn to the left so begin at the left side and use upward strokes

THE OGHAM

The Aicme Muin:
> draws its lines diagonally across both sides of the edge so use across/intersecting strokes

The Aicme Ailim:
> crossed lines or notches are vowels drawn either as short marks on the edge itself, or straight across both sides of the edge.

Ogham is also known as Ogham Craobh (tree ogham) or Beith-Luis-Nuin, after the letter names of the first letters in the same manner as the Greek letters Alpha and Beta form the word alphabet. The word Nuin literally means a forked branch or a written letter of the Ogham, so Beith-Luis-Nuin translates to the Beith-Luis letters.

The trees of the Ogham alphabet are further divided into four ranks where Chieftains rank first, followed by Peasants who are the sentries and servants of the chieftain trees, Shrubs who are earth healing trees rank third and finally the Brambles are an extension of the caring, conditioning and healing of the shrub trees:

Chieftain trees:
> Oaks, Ash, Hazels, Apple, Holly, Pines and Yews

Peasant trees:
> Alders, Willows, Hawthorns, Rowans, Birches, Beeches, and Elms

Shrubs:
> Blackthorns, Elders and Poplars

Brambles:
> Ivy, Heather, Reeds, Gorse, and Vines

THE OGHAM

The Forfeda

Around the 4th century five additional feda called the Forfeda were added to the original twenty to supplement the written Ogham. These are:

> Chelwydd (Mistletoe)
> Oir (Spindle)
> Uilleand (Honeysuckle)
> Iphin (Gooseberry)
> Eamancholl (Beech)

The Forfeda are arranged in their own aicme and like the original Ogham, there are a number of versions of the Forfeda. Some Forfeda include the letter P, which was originally the NG of Ngetal in one of the earlier Ogham.

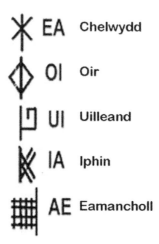

EA   Chelwydd

OI   Oir

UI   Uilleand

IA   Iphin

AE   Eamancholl

Ogham feda, their stories, spiritual and medicinal uses

Ogham is a twenty feda language developed for the Primitive Irish (with five feda added in the 4th century) which was the ancestor to the better-known Old Irish, which is the ancestor of all three contemporary Gaelic languages (Irish, Manx, and Scottish Gaelic).

The Ogham was oral until the 12th century, when written Irish Gaelic became the language of a great literature[5] ultimately transcribed by monks. Ogham can be fun, used through the centuries for ciphers and codes by ingenious Medieval minds and it may be that the cryptic varieties[6] were studied as a way to train the mind in the use of words and concepts[7].

Although each feda has its own story, traditional spiritual and medicinal uses and energy please be mindful that these stories are offered for your interest only. If you seek cures, it is wiser not to self-medicate but instead see your doctor, herbalist or naturopath. Although tree medicine is natural it is not harmless and should be approached with prudent respect and cautious awe.

---

[5] Including The Book of the Dun Cow
[6] See Appendix 2: Ogham Etymology & Variations
[7] The old manuscripts list numerous categories including Saints, dogs, art, rivers and cows as types of Ogham, see Appendix 2.

THE OGHAM

Beith (Birch)

Birch is a broad-leaved deciduous hardwood tree of the genus Betula which also includes alders and hazels and is sometimes called *"the watchful tree"* because of eye-like impressions on the bark. Birch trees have thin papery bark that peels easily so birds use it to build their nests. In Ireland, the first Ogham was written on birch which is why it became known as the tree of tutelage.

Birch tea made from either leaves or twigs is a laxative and healing to mouth sores, kidney and bladder sediments, and gout. The tea also helps to ease rheumatic pains. Modern medicine confirms that betulinic acid, formed in birch sap, discourages tumours and cancer. Dry distillation of fresh birch wood gives a tar which can be used as an ointment for skin irritations. The leaves are best when gathered in spring, and the oil is tapped at the end of winter.

The Celts also associated the birch with love and many love poems are about the birch which is also known as Lady of the Woods, Paper Birch and White Birch. If you want to find love, carefully gather strips of the bark at the New Moon and write with red ink on a birch strip *"Bring me true love."* Burn this along with a love incense, saying *"Goddess of love, God of desire, bring to me sweet passion's fire"* then wait to see who comes as your perfect mate.

Please remember that it is unwise to use this incantation and ritual directed toward a specific person as that would violate their personal space. If true love is to come to you, it must be of that person's free will to do so.

THE OGHAM

Birch symbolises cleanliness and determination to overcome adversity. This is good energy to make fresh starts and to rid yourself of bad influences.

Birch attributes in brief are:
>Time of influence: 24 December/20 January
>Colour: White
>Rank: Chieftain
>Letter: B
>Element: Air
>Personality Opposites: Happy/immature

Luis (Rowan)

Rowans are small, sturdy trees with compound leaves of up to seventeen leaflets and spring clusters of white flowers with five petals.

Red rowan berries are bitter, astringent, and very high in Vitamin C. They should be picked just after the first frost when their colour has deepened. They are a mild purgative, diuretic and general tonic, also useful in the treatment of constipation and kidney disorders. One of the sugars in the fruit can used for glaucoma, and sorbose which is a diabetic sweetener is made from rowan berries. Rowan berries may be added to ales and cordials. The old Scots made a syrup for coughs and colds from rowan berries, apples, and honey.

The Gaelic for rowan, Luis, also means flame, hand, branch, mantle or pure which is why the rowan is associated with the Irish goddess, Brigid or Bride and is sacred to the Druids.

THE OGHAM

Rowan is placed over barns and byres to protect against evil influences, and rowan guards the gateway to the spirit world. Rowan can also protect against lightning strike.

This tree is also known as Mountain Ash, Witchwood and Sorb Apple and helps to protect against enchantment and beguiling. Rowan branches are used to carve Omen Sticks to use in divination. Wands made from the rowan are used for knowledge, locating metal and general divination.

Rowan's attributes in brief are:
> Time of influence: 21January/17 February
> Colour: Gray and red
> Rank: Shrub
> Letter: L
> Element: Air
> Personality opposites: Spiritual/Fanatical

Fearn (Alder)
Fearn is a small tree that thrives in damp areas such as wetlands and river banks. It usually has several greyish trunks and its female catkins develop into what look like tiny brown pine cones.

Alder bark is simmered in water to make a healing wash for deep wounds as it is astringent and can help to pull the edges of a wound together. A tea made from the leaves and bark may benefit tonsillitis and fever. The leaves are also used in poultices to dry up breast milk. Alder bark tea can be used as a douche or for haemorrhoids. Fresh sap can be applied to any area to relieve itching.

THE OGHAM

Fearn was one of the nine sacred woods used to kindle the Beltaine fire. The word fearn can also mean a shield that protects against negative emotions. This tree is sacred to the Druids and as the pith is easily pushed out of green shoots to make whistles, you can bind several shoots together and trim them to the right length to produce the note you need to call the Air elementals. Alder is a tree used for spiritual protection and of prophecy.

The god linked with this tree is Bran the Blessed who is a king and a giant in Welsh mythology. Bran is son to Llyr and the brother of Branwen, Manawydan, Nisien and Efnysien.

Alder attributes in brief are:
> Time of influence: 18 March/14 April
> Colour: Crimson
> Rank: Chieftain
> Letter: F, V
> Element: Fire
> Personality opposites: Ambitious/impulsive

Saille (Willow)

The Willow is sacred to the Moon, and Celtic myth says that the universe hatched from two crimson serpent's eggs which were protected by a Willow tree.

Willows are water-loving trees with slender flexible twigs and long, narrow leaves. The golden willow catkins bloom in early spring then the catkins mature into small seed capsules in late summer.

THE OGHAM

All willow barks produce salicylic acid which is a natural aspirin. Willow bark tea is used to treat muscle pain and inflammation, diarrhoea, fever, arthritic pain, and headache. Used externally willow makes a wash to treat cuts, ulcers, and poison ivy. Willow bark in teas and capsules is sedative and eases insomnia. Willow reduces the risk of heart disease and may delay cataract formation. Willow is also known as White Willow, Tree of Enchantment and Witches' Aspirin.

Willow is one of the seven sacred trees of the Irish and is a tree sacred to the Druids. Priests, priestesses and artisans sat in willow groves to gain eloquence, inspiration, skills and prophecies. For a wish to be granted first ask the willow for permission and for help to select a pliable shoot. Tie a loose knot in the shoot while telling the willow of your wish. When the wish is fulfilled go back and untie the knot. Remember to thank the willow and leave a gift.

Willow attributes in brief are:
>Time of influence: 15 April/12 May
>Colour: Shown only as bright
>Rank: Chieftain
>Letter: S
>Element: Water
>Personality opposites: Wise/bitter

THE OGHAM

Nuin (Ash)

Ash is a tall tree with compound leaves and bark that is tightly and regularly furrowed. Its seeds hang in clusters until they turn brown and drop off in the autumn.

In medicine, both the bark and leaves of ash are mildly laxative and diuretic. The leaves are gathered in summer and the bark in spring. An ash infusion can regulate bowel movements, expel intestinal parasites, reduce fever, treat kidney and urinary infections and alleviate rheumatic and gout pains. Externally the leaves are used in compresses or in the bath to treat weeping wounds.

In Norse mythology the *"World Tree"* was a giant ash, and three ash trees are among the five magical trees planted by Fintan in Ireland. In Irish mythology Fintan known as *"the Wise"* is a seer who escorted Noah's granddaughter Cessair to Ireland before the deluge. His wives and children were drowned when the flood arrived but he survived in the form of a salmon, then turned into an eagle and then a hawk before he changed back to human form.

Fintan lived for 5,500 years after the deluge, surviving into the time of Fionn mac Cumhail and becoming the fountain of all knowledge and all history along with a magical hawk who was born at the same time as him. When they meet at the end of their lives they decide to leave the mortal realm together sometime in the 5th century, after Ireland was converted to Christianity.

The ash is symbolic of the warrior, and represents the need for strength and control in life on all levels, where you accept responsibility for your own actions and situation even if you are under threat. Druid wands are often made of ash because of its straight grain. Ash wands are good for healing and for general magic.

Put fresh ash leaves under your pillow to encourage psychic dreams. Ash helps us to link the earthly and spiritual, yourself and the cosmos, lowest and highest. The ash is good energy for meditation and multi-dimensional travel.

Ash attributes in brief are:
> Time of influence: 18 February/17 March
> Colour: Glass green
> Rank: Peasant
> Letter: N
> Element: Air
> Personality opposites: Charming/egocentric

Huatha (Hawthorn)

Hawthorn is a small, broad and dense tree with thorns and edible red fruits. The hawthorn's autumn berries and spring new leaves and flowers make a cardiac tonic that benefits most heart conditions. Herbalists recommend use only for a few weeks before taking a week off to prevent a steep drop in blood pressure and warn to use caution when combining this herb with other heart medications to prevent a sudden drop in blood pressure.

If you are prescribed a hawthorn treatment by your doctor or herbalist, check with them if you should also eat fresh raw garlic for maximum benefit because garlic will cleanse plaque in the blood vessels.

THE OGHAM

The sharp-thorned hawthorn is a symbol of psychic protection and in the northern hemisphere, hawthorn is in blossom for Beltaine, the Celtic fire festival celebrating the time of the rising of the Sun and the running of the deer.

Hawthorn is also known as May Tree and White Thorn and is used for protection, love and marriage spells. Faeries live in hawthorn so hawthorn hedges are planted around fields, houses and churchyards to protect them. Wands made of this wood have great power. The blossoms are highly erotic to men but this tree is best used for cleansing and chastity, bringing protection from the inner magical realms.

Hawthorn attributes in brief are:
       Time of influence: 13 May/9 June
       Colour: Purple
       Rank: Peasant
       Letter: H
       Element: Fire
       Personality opposites: Passionate/ruthless

Duir (Oak)

Oaks are large trees with acorns topped by bowl-shaped caps. The best oak for internal use is White Oak, though all oaks are valuable as external washes. The tannins in oak bark and leaves help to pull the edges of a wound together and are antiseptic and antiviral. White Oak bark tea is used for chronic diarrhoea, chronic mucus discharges, and piles. It makes a gargle for sore throats and washes for skin problems such as poison ivy, burns and wounds. A tea made from the leaf or the bark is used by women as a douche for vaginitis. Be aware that prolonged consumption can be harmful.

THE OGHAM

Oak is an important symbol in Druidic lore as it is strong, tall and very long-lived. The oak is one of the sacred trees, symbolising truth and steadfast knowledge. Oak doors will keep out evil and wands are made of its wood.

The oak is the "*King of Trees*" and is held sacred by many cultures. The Celts held the oak in particular esteem because of its size, longevity, and nutritious acorns.

Acorns are gathered at night for the greatest fertility and the old ones listened to the rustling oak leaves and the wrens in the trees for divinatory messages. Burning oak leaves purifies the atmosphere and oak can be used in spells for protection, strength, success and stability. Oak energy will protect you so you can focus while you pursue your goals and is essential protection for those less able and weaker, who need a safe place while they work to strengthen their characters.

Oak attributes in brief are:
>   Time of influence: 10 June/7 July
>   Colour: Black and dark brown
>   Rank: Chieftain
>   Letter: D
>   Element: Fire
>   Personality opposites: Fatherly/dominating

THE OGHAM

Tinne (Holly)

English holly or European holly is a familiar evergreen usually seen as decoration for the northern Yule. It has spiny oval leaves and shiny red berries. Although the leaves can be used as a tea substitute and in infusions for coughs, colds and flu, please be aware that the berries of all holly varieties are strong purgatives.

When Celtic chieftains are chosen by the tribe their first crown is a holly wreath because holly will repel enemies.

Holly is a beautiful white wood with an almost invisible grain and looks like ivory.

Holly symbolises the death and rebirth of winter in both Pagan and Christian lore and is important to the Winter Solstice. In Arthurian legend, Gawain as the *"Oak King of Summer"* fought the *"Green Knight"* who was armed with a holly club to represent winter.

Holly is used in spells for sleep or rest and to ease the passage of death. A bag of holly leaves and berries carried by a man is believed to increase his ability to attract women.

Holly attributes in brief are:
> Time of influence: 8 July/4 August
> Colour: Dark Grey
> Rank: Shrub
> Letter: T
> Element: Fire
> Personality opposites: Determined/Insensitive

THE OGHAM

Coll (Hazel)

The hazel is a genus of deciduous trees and large shrubs native to the temperate Northern Hemisphere. Hazels have simple, rounded leaves with double-serrated edges.

The flowers appear very early in spring before the leaves. The male catkins are pale yellow and 5–12 cm long and the female catkins are very small and often concealed in the buds. The fruit of the hazel is the hazelnut, which grow two to four in a cluster.

Hazelnuts are believed to benefit the kidneys. Huron herbalists used the bark in poultices for tumours and ulcers. The Iroquois mixed the nut oil with bear's grease to make mosquito repellent. The Chippewa used a decoction of hazel root, White Oak root, chokecherry bark and the heartwood or ironwood to treat bleeding from the lungs.

Hazel is the easiest tree to find in Celtic legends and each tree carries both male and female flowers. It is known as Bile Ratha or *"the sacred / venerated tree of the Rath (or the place of the Sidhe or faeries)"*.

If you need wisdom you should eat the nuts of the hazel, and if you are in need of inspiration go fishing in a pool using a hazel rod with a rowan berry tied to a line to use as bait.

Hazel twigs are traditionally used by dowsers to find hidden water or buried treasure. Wands made of this wood are good for healing. To ask for help from the plant faeries, string hazelnuts on a cord and hang them in your house or ritual room. Hazel wood can be used to gain knowledge, wisdom and poetic inspiration.

THE OGHAM

Hazel attributes in brief are:
        Time of influence: 5 August to 1 September
        Colour: Brown
        Rank: Shrub
        Letter: C, K
        Element: Water
        Personality opposites: Generous/deceptive

Quert (Apple)

Apples grow on deciduous trees which are large if grown from seed, but small if grafted onto roots of other trees as rootstock. The tree originated in central Asia where its wild ancestor is still found today. Apples have grown for thousands of years in Asia and Europe, and were brought to North America by European colonists. Apples feature in the mythology and religions of many cultures including the Norse, Greek and Christian traditions.

Apples are rich in magnesium, iron, potassium, and vitamins C, B and B2. When peeled of their skin and eaten raw apples may relieve diarrhoea while stewed unpeeled apples are a laxative. Eating apples regularly promotes restful sleep. Baked apples can be applied warm as a poultice for sore throats and fevers. Raw apple cider will restore the correct bacteria to the bowels after a course of antibiotics. Apples reduce acidity in the stomach and help to clean the liver. Garlic and horseradish were added to apple cider and the mixture used as a wash externally and taken internally as a drink to clear the skin. The bark of the root of apple trees is used for fevers.

THE OGHAM

In Celtic tradition, the apple is associated with the Otherworld. The woman who guides you to the *"Lands of Promise"* or to the *"Isles of Women"* always carries a sacred apple branch. The Mother aspect of the Triple Goddess is often found in an apple orchard and faeries know when a powerful Druid is near, because his approach is heralded by the ringing of silver bells tied to an apple branch.

The custom of dooking for apples in water at Samhainn symbolises our ambitions; some we achieve, some we don't.
Apple is another tree sacred to the Druids and you can substitute apple cider for blood or wine in any old spells. Apple indicates choice and is useful for love and healing magic. The choice you may have to make is often between similar and equally attractive things. This is good energy to use when you have difficulty in making decisions in your life whether they are work or relationship oriented.

Apple attributes in brief are:
>   Time of influence: The light half of the year
>   Colour: Green
>   Rank: Chieftain
>   Letter: Q
>   Element: Water
>   Personality opposites: Motherly/Weak-willed

THE OGHAM

Muin (Vine)

A vine usually means the grapevine but can also mean any plant with trailing or climbing stems. The word can also refer to the stems used in wicker work.

Vines when unchecked can strangle even the largest tree, and carry a lesson about restriction and what can happen to us spiritually if we allow too many things to pile up and entwine around us. We can allow outer issues to hinder the development of our spiritual life, small things like constant drains on our time or things that cloud our inner vision (like consumerism and politics). Vines remind us to guard the trees of our inner sacred grove from things and people that can drain our energy. The best use for vine energy is when you want to reach a deeper state of consciousness or when doing healing work on others.

The vine needs loving care to bear fruit in the cooler Celtic climate and so became a symbol of sacred knowledge and spiritual initiation and is used in the development of prophetic powers.

Vine attributes in brief are:
> Time of influence: 2 to 29 September
> Colour: Variegated
> Rank: Bramble
> Letter: M
> Element: Water
> Personality opposites: Sympathetic/dependent

THE OGHAM

Gort (Ivy)

Ivy is a genus of 12–15 species of evergreen climbing or ground-creeping woody plants native to western, central and southern Europe, north-western Africa and across central-southern Asia east to Japan and Taiwan. On level ground they remain a low plant but on suitable surfaces for climbing such as trees, rocks or buildings they can climb up to 30 metres above the ground.

Ivy has two leaf types to show if it is a juvenile or an adult plant. The flowers are greenish-yellow with five small petals produced in autumn to early winter and are very rich in nectar. The fruit is a greenish-black, dark purple or yellow berry, ripening in late winter to mid-spring. Ivy seeds are dispersed by birds when they eat the berries.
The power of ivy to cling and to bind makes it a potent symbol of determination and strength. Ivy can strangle trees so has become a sign of death and spiritual growth.

Ivy's circular climb represents the spiral of the self and the search for self-knowledge. The maze of the labyrinth is also like the ivy since it also symbolizes the wandering of the soul as you circle and seek before leading you to enlightenment in the centre of the maze. Ivy is a good aid if you help others on a spiritual journey.

Ivy attributes in brief are:
>Time of influence: 30 September/27 October
>Colour: Sky blue
>Rank: Bramble
>Letter: G
>Element: Earth
>Personality opposites: Ambitious/lazy

THE OGHAM

Ngetal (Reed)

Reed is a common name for several tall, grass-like plants that grow in wetlands. Paper reed or papyrus is the ancient Egyptian writing material, which is also used for making boats. The common reed in Britain is used in many areas for thatching roofs and known as "*Norfolk reed*" or "*water reed*". Roof thatch known as "*wheat reed*" or "*Devon reed*" are not reeds, but long-stemmed wheat straw.

The Celts believed the reed was a tree because of its dense root system. Because cut reeds were used as pens, reeds symbolise wisdom and scholarship.

Reed helps create spiritual weapons and gives you direction. Reed energy is good to use before beginning healing work or working on soul retrievals for others.

Reed attributes in brief are:
> Time of influence: 28 October/24 November
> Colour: Grass green
> Rank: Bramble
> Letter: NG
> Element: Air
> Personality opposites: Adaptable/Indecisive

THE OGHAM

Straif (Blackthorn)

Blackthorn is a large deciduous shrub or small tree growing to 5 metres tall with blackish bark and dense spiny branches. The leaves are oval and the flowers have five creamy-white petals which grow in early spring.

The fruit is called a "*sloe*" and is black, ripening in autumn to be harvested in the UK in October or November after the first frosts. The common name "*blackthorn*" describes the thorny shrub and the very dark bark.

Blackthorn fruit or sloes are used in preserves but can be too tart unless picked within a few days of autumn frost. The juice is used to make wine or sloe gin.

Sloes preserved in vinegar are similar in taste to Japanese umeboshi or salt plums. The juice of the berries dyes linen a reddish colour that washes out to a durable pale blue.

Evidence of the early use of sloes by man was shown in the 5,300-year-old human mummy discovered in 1991 in the Austrian-Italian Alps which still had undigested sloes in the stomach contents. A "*sloe-thorn worm*" used as fishing bait is mentioned in the 15th century *"The Treatyse of Fishing"* written by Juliana Berners.

Blackthorn makes an excellent fire wood that burns slowly with a good heat and little smoke. The wood takes a fine polish and straight Blackthorn stems are traditionally made into tool handles, walking sticks or clubs. In the British Army, commissioned officers of the Royal Irish Regiment carry Blackthorn sticks. Blackthorn wood is used to make the cudgel called a shillelagh as well as the Druid's Blasting Stick.

THE OGHAM

Blackthorn is a winter tree with vicious thorns and grows in dense thickets and was used in Northern Europe and Britain to make "cattle-proof" hedges to keep cows from roaming.

Blackthorn indicates strong action of fate or outside influences that must be obeyed. Use Blackthorn during times when you face problems that seem insurmountable. Although Blackthorn may help you to conquer problems always use it with caution and respect remembering that the Gaelic word "*straif*" has links with the English word "*strife*".

Blackthorn attributes in brief are:

        Time of influence: The dark half of the year
        Colour: Purple
        Rank: Shrub
        Letter: SS, Z, ST
        Element: Earth
        Personality opposites: Honest/Deceptive

Ruis (Elder)

Elder trees are small with clusters of white flowers in spring and black or deep purple berries in autumn. They thrive in damp, moist areas.

Elderberries are used to make preserves, pies, and wine. Fresh or dried berries make a tea to benefit the lungs and nourish the blood. The young leaves of elder make salves and poultices for skin healing. A tea made from root bark clears congestion, eases headaches, and is used in poultices for mastitis. A tincture of the flowers lowers fever by promoting perspiration. Elderflower water is a traditional remedy for skin blemishes and sunburn. Cold elderflower tea is a soothing compress for inflammation of the eyes. Elderflower oil makes a soothing balm for sore nipples of nursing mothers.

Elder trees are sacred to the faeries and branches of elder are hung above stables to protect the horses. It is unlucky to burn elder and an omen of death to bring it indoors. Remember the words of the Rede: *"Elder is the Lady's Tree, burn it not or cursed ye be"*.

Elder is also known as Elkhorn, Elderberry and Lady Elder and is sacred to the White Lady and Midsummer Solstice. The Druids used it to both bless and curse. Standing under an elder tree at Midsummer is similar to standing in a Faery Ring of mushrooms and will help you clear your vision to see the faeries. Elder wands can be used to drive out evil spirits.

This tree is linked to the eternal wheel of life and death, birth and rebirth. It represents the end which is the beginning and the beginning which is the end. Elder signifies creativity and renewal and new beginnings.

Elder attributes in brief are:
        Time of influence: 25 November/23 December
        Colour: Red
        Rank: Shrub
        Letter: R
        Element: Earth
        Personality opposites: Intelligent/Unfortunate

THE OGHAM

Ailim (Pine or Silver Fir)

Pines are coniferous evergreens with needles that grow in soft clusters and are recognized worldwide as healing agents. Any pine or evergreen such as Spruce, Larch or Cedar has antiseptic properties so is useful as a wound wash.

The most palatable pine for internal use is the White Pine whose needles and twigs makes a tea that is rich in vitamin C and useful for sore throats, coughs, and colds. Pine tea also makes a relaxing foot bath. Pine baths aid kidney ailments, improve circulation, and are relaxing to sore muscles. The smell of pine soothes the nerves and lungs.

Pine is known to the Druids as one of the seven trees of the Irish and its old title was *"the sweetest of woods"*. Mix the dried needles of pine with equal parts of juniper and cedar and burn to purify the home and ritual area. The cones and nuts can be carried as a fertility charm.

A good cleansing and stimulating bath can be made by placing pine needles in a loose-woven bag and running bath water over it. To purify and sanctify an outdoor ritual area, brush the ground with a pine branch.

The Silver Fir can bring the knowledge of both your present and past lives together into the "*now*"; helps with awareness of progress on your spiritual journey.

Silver Fir is good energy to use on your search for the gift of insight.

THE OGHAM

Pine attributes in brief are:

      Time of influence: second day of Winter Solstice
      Colour: Light blue
      Rank: Peasant
      Letter: A
      Element: Earth
      Personality opposites: Outgoing/Introverted

Ohn (Furze)

Furse is also known as gorse and whin and its golden flowers herald the Spring Equinox. Both wood and blooms are burned for protection and in preparation for conflict of any sort. Although it looks sturdy, furse is not very hardy and can be injured by severe frost.

Furse blossoms all year round, hence the old saying: *"When gorse is out of bloom, kissing is out of season"* which led to inserting a spray of gorse in the bridal bouquet.

Old writers tell us that *"sodden with honey, it clears the mouth"* and that it *"is good against snake-bite"*. Furse also has an old reputation as an insecticide: *"Against fleas, take this same wort, with its seed, sodden; sprinkle it into the house; it killeth the fleas."*

Furse attributes in brief are:

      Time of influence: Spring Equinox
      Colour: Yellow gold
      Rank: Bramble
      Letter: O
      Element: Fire
      Personality opposites: Prosperous/Vain

THE OGHAM

Ur (Heather)

Heather is a low-growing perennial shrub found across Europe and Asia Minor that flowers in late summer and regenerates easily even when grazed often. This trait makes heather a dominant plant in heathland and moorland, as well as in some bogs and woodland.

Heather wildflowers are normally mauve, but white-flowered plants grow occasionally. White heather is regarded in Scotland as being lucky, a tradition brought from Balmoral to England by Queen Victoria and sprigs of it are often sold as a charm and used in bridal bouquets.

Heather is used to dye wool yellow, to tan leather and to make heather beer. Thomas Pennant wrote in 1769 that on the Scottish island of Islay *"ale is frequently made of the young tops of heath, mixing two thirds of that plant with one of malt, sometimes adding hops"*.

Heather has been used in traditional Austrian medicine internally as a tea for treatment of disorders of the kidneys and urinary tract. From ancient times heather was used for making besoms, or brooms.

Heather honey is a highly valued product of both moorland and heathland areas, with a characteristic strong taste and an unusual texture because it is thixotropic, being a jelly until stirred when it turns into a syrup. When allowed to settle, heather honey reverts to being a jelly. This property makes the extraction of heather honey from the comb difficult, so it is often sold as comb honey.

THE OGHAM

Useful for going within in solitary healing work, heather along with mistletoe create a powerful healing medicine both spiritually and physically. Heather is used today in some alternative medicines as a treatment for cancer.

Heather attributes in brief are:
> Time of influence: Midsummer
> Colour: Purple
> Rank: Bramble
> Letter: U
> Element: Air
> Personality opposites: Carefree/Superficial

Eadha (Aspen or White Poplar)

Poplars are known by their drooping catkins and rounded leaves with pointed tips. The sticky spring buds are gathered in May and are used in salves for skin problems, sprains, sore muscles, wounds, headaches, tumours, eczema, bruises, gout, and on the chest for lung ailments and coughs.

The buds are used internally for phlegm, kidney and bladder ailments, coughs, scurvy, and rheumatic pains. The root was combined with the root of White Poplar in a decoction to stop premature bleeding in pregnancy. The warmed juice of White Poplar was used for sore ears.

Poplar barks are high in salicin which makes them useful in treating deep wounds, gangrene, eczema, cancer, burns, and strong body odour. The inner bark of a young poplar tree is edible in the spring and can be simmered into a tea for liver and kidney ailments.

THE OGHAM

Poplars are spectacular trees with a very strong set of roots, which affords them the symbolic value of grounding, security and resiliency. Poplar is useful for manifestation, vibrating with strong Earth energy associated with finances, providence and overcoming blockages. This tree is useful when considering earthly and material aspects of life. It also helps to find the spiritual determination to face the hardships that we endure through life.

The Poplar tree has the ability to resist and to shield, a kinship with languages and speech, and a close relationship with the winds. Listen to the wind through the Poplar tree to get messages from past lives.

Poplar attributes in brief are:
        Time of influence: Autumn Equinox
        Colour: Silver white
        Rank: Peasant
        Letter: E
        Element: Water
        Personality opposites: Caring/Insecure

Ioho (Yew)

Yew grows into a very tall tree and with age forms a very stout trunk covered with red-brown, peeling bark and topped with a wide spread of branches. The yew is famous in the history and legends of Great Britain. To the Druids the yew was a sacred tree, a custom adopted by the early Christians so the yew is still associated with places of worship as well as the Winter Solstice and the deities of death and rebirth.

THE OGHAM

Yew wood is beautifully smooth and golden with a wavy grain. The Irish use it to make dagger handles, bows and wine barrels. The wood or leaves are laid on graves as a reminder to the departed spirit that death is only a pause in the life cycle before rebirth. All parts of the tree are poisonous except the fleshy covering of the berry. Many cattle have been poisoned from eating yew. The yew is good when working with past life issues and regression.

Yew attributes in brief are:
>Time of influence: Midwinter solstice
>Colour: Dark green
>Rank: Peasant
>Letter: I, J, Y
>Element: Earth
>Personality opposites: Enduring/Sanguine

Chelwydd (Mistletoe)

Mistletoe is an evergreen parasitic plant growing on the branches of host trees including apple, ash, hawthorn, lime and sometimes oak. Mistletoe is also known as Birdlime, All Heal and Golden Bough. Although the berries are poisonous they are used in love incenses. Bunches of mistletoe are hung as an all-purpose protective herb.

Mistletoe was held in great reverence by the Druids and harvested with great ceremony at a particular time of the moon. If the mistletoe was not harvested and fell to the ground, it was an omen of misfortune. Mistletoe protects from all evil and is used to announce the entrance of the New Year. Using it as a Christmas decoration is a survival of this old custom, because mistletoe rules the Winter Solstice.

THE OGHAM

Oir (Spindle)

Spindle is a deciduous flowering small tree or shrub native to Europe and is a popular ornamental plant in gardens throughout the world so is now found wild throughout North and Central America, Europe, Asia, Africa, and Australia. Other names include Fusoria, Fusanum, Ananbeam, Shemshad Rasmi, Prickwood, Skewerwood and Pincushion Shrub. It is a food plant of the Holly Blue butterfly as well as a favourite tree of robins, so much so that it is also known as Robins' Bread.

The serrated leaves are dark green in summer and yellow green to reddish purple in autumn. The spring flowers are yellow green and the fruit ripens in autumn to red, purple or pink, splitting open to reveal orange seeds when ripe.

William Turner (1508 – 1568) the radical Protestant cleric who wrote *"A New Herball"* is believed to have christened the tree *'Spindle Tree'* saying: *"I coulde never learne an Englishe name for it. The Duche men call it in Netherlande, spilboome, that is, spindel-tree, because they use to make spindels of it in that country, and me thynke it may be as well named in English seying we have no other name. I know no goode propertie that this tree hath, saving only it is good to make spindels and brid of cages[8]."*

Parts of the plant have been used medicinally. The resin Euonymin made from the bark stimulates the appetite and is useful in the treatment of liver disorders which accompany fevers but in larger doses will irritate the intestine and is cathartic. The seeds are a strong emetic and purgative. The

---

[8] bird-cages

fresh leaves and the dried fruit and seeds are used externally to treat scabies, lice, ticks and other skin parasites. Great care should be taken because most of the plant is poisonous and the fruit is very dangerous resulting in poisonings in children and grazing animals who are attracted by the brightly coloured fruit.

Other uses for spindle include dyes, insecticide, and a volatile oil that is used to make soap. Because the very hard, easily split and fine-grained wood was used for spindles, skewers, knitting needles, toothpicks and to make a smooth charcoal preferred by artists, spindle came to symbolize creative inspiration, purification, initiation and blessings. This plant reminds us that for every action there is an equal and opposite reaction, or that things change from positive to negative depending on how you use them.

Spindle reminds us of the honour of tribe, community and the sweetness and delight of a sudden revelation. Physically we should fulfil obligations, not for reward but because the greatest happiness will be yours knowing you have done what is right. Mentally, Spindle brings a sudden realization that gives you the right and obligation to question authority. Spiritually, Spindle develops your consciousness of the right relationship with others in the community and tribe.

Robert Graves says that the Spindle is represented in Manannan's crane bag as the King of Lochlainn's helmet. Due to its name it can be also related to any of the spinning and weaving mythology found around the globe.

THE OGHAM

Uilleand (Honeysuckle)

Honeysuckles are shrubs or vines native to the northern hemisphere with sweet-scented clusters of flowers that produce edible nectar. The stringy stems are useful for binding and textiles. The fruit is a red, blue or black berry containing several seeds which are mildly poisonous even though they are attractive to wildlife. A dozen or more species of honeysuckle are used medicinally, the fruits generally having both emetic and cathartic properties. The native English honeysuckle is both an expectorant and a laxative. Syrup made from flowers is used for diseases of the respiratory organs and in asthma and the leaves as decoction in diseases of the liver and spleen. It was also used in gargles.

Nicholas Culpeper says: "*Honeysuckles are cleansing, consuming and digesting, and therefore no way fit for inflammations. It is fitting a conserve made of the flowers should be kept in every gentlewoman's house; I know no better cure for the asthma than this besides it takes away the evil of the spleen: provokes urine, procures speedy delivery of women in travail, relieves cramps, convulsions, and palsies, and whatsoever griefs come of cold or obstructed perspiration; if you make use of it as an ointment, it will clear the skin of morphew, freckles, and sunburnings, or whatever else discolours it, and then the maids will love it.*"

Honeysuckle helps you to distinguish what is real and what is false and what is of true value. The honeysuckle will help you to tread safely while you remain true to your ideals and principles. While ivy with its inward spiral spins its way to inner knowledge, honeysuckle shows the way outwards. Robert Graves connects the honeysuckle cross to the bones of the whale in the crane-bag of Mannanan.

THE OGHAM

Iphin (Gooseberry)

Gooseberry is native to Europe, northwest Africa, west, south and southeast Asia and gooseberry bushes produce an edible fruit grown both on a commercial and domestic basis. The gooseberry is a sprawling bush with branches thickly set with sharp spines. The flowers are bell-shaped and the fruit are berries, smaller in the wild than the cultivated varieties. The berries are usually green, but there are also red, purple, yellow, and white varieties.

Gooseberries are used as an ingredient in desserts such as pies, fools and crumbles. They are also used to flavour beverages such as sodas, flavoured waters, or milk, and can be made into fruit wines and teas. Gooseberries can be preserved as jams or dried fruit and were popular in the United Kingdom before fruit was imported as they are the first available fresh fruit of the year. Gooseberry growing was very popular in the 19th century and William Turner describes the gooseberry in his 16th century herbal.

A jelly made from the gooseberry berries aids digestive problems and helps reduce fevers. A tincture or tea made from the gooseberry leaves helps with pre-menstrual problems. Lady Wilde in Ancient Legends, Mystic Charms & Superstitions of Ireland, 1887 recommends *"To rid a sty that has developed on the eyelid, point a gooseberry thorn at it and say "away, away, away."*

"*Gooseberry bush*" was 19th century slang for pubic hair and from this comes the saying that babies are "*Born under a gooseberry bush*" which complements the Victorian flower meaning of the gooseberry blossom as *"anticipation"*.

THE OGHAM

In the newspaper business the phrase *"great gooseberry season"* is used to describe a period where there isn't much headline news so stories about the largest gooseberry are published instead. The phrase *"playing gooseberry"* means a third person and possible chaperone of a group where the other two people are courting, a reference to the chaperone often pretending to pick fruit in order to give the courting couple some privacy. The phrase *"going gooseberrying"* involves stealing clothes that are hanging to dry.

Gooseberry is said to have sympathetic magical qualities, representing that which is tasteful and the divine influence. Gooseberry is not often found in folklore but has a strong association with fairies. It is connected with both the *"dance of life"* as well as the *"mystic crane dance"* performed through labyrinths.

Eamancholl (Beech)

Beech is a deciduous tree with both male and female flowers on the same plant native to temperate Europe, Asia and North America. Beech only arrived in Great Britain after the last ice age and although is classified as a native in the south of England it is a non-native in the north and in Ireland. It produces small edible nuts with a high tannin content which makes them bitter and are called beechnuts or beechmast, which has a high fat content so can be pressed for edible oil.

The tree canopy casts dense shade and carpets the ground with dense leaf litter. Fresh beech leaves are a fine salad vegetable, soft in texture and as sweet as a mild cabbage. Young leaves steeped in gin for several weeks and sweetened produce a light green/yellow liqueur.

THE OGHAM

Beech wood is excellent firewood because it is easily split and burns for many hours. Budweiser beer uses beech wood and burned beech logs are used to dry the malts used in some German smoked beers, as well as being used to smoke Westphalian ham and some sausages and cheeses.

Beech trees have a distinctive, smooth grey bark that looks like elephant skin. This bark is extremely thin and scars easily so carvings such as lovers' initials and other graffiti remain because the tree is unable to heal itself. The bark is used as a tea for lung problems. It is also cleansing to the blood, though pregnant women should avoid it. Beech bark tea makes a good wash for poison ivy. Beech leaves are used in poultices for burns and frostbite, and can be used to reduce swelling. Bach Flower Remedies use beech to counteract mental rigidity, fault finding, intolerance, arrogance and lack of sympathy.

Beech is about language, literature and books, the workings of destiny, as well as pure desire and pleasure. Beech energy can tell you much about yesterday and how it is relevant today. Use Beech when you handle old objects or visit a place connected with your past to bring understanding of people and incidents, reviving the memories within you that you need. Graves sees this Forfeda as meaning the Sea, which represents that which is other or otherworldly. In the Celtic Tree Oracle Liz and Colin Murray link Beech to the physical ocean, travel and maternal links and say this feda means *"hidden knowledge that is only available when the moon and sea are full."*

Ogham Music

You need a collection of sounds to create a language, but the Celts are unusual in that they sang their Ogham rather than just speaking their words.

Every symbol of the Ogham alphabet has its own note that was sung each time the symbol was used, so even when the Ogham became a written language or was used as hand signals every listener could "*hear*" the exact message in their mind. Through using the Ogham symbols to inspire the chanting of words, the words themselves affect the listener because music alters our reception and perception.

Music is a universal language used to celebrate or to grieve, to rouse to battle or soothe to sleep, which could be why the Ogham is such a powerful language that has endured through so many centuries. Our lack of such a language with such a depth of meanings could also be why there is so much misunderstanding today on social media because what may be written with the intent of humour can be read as rudeness, depending on how the reader "*hears*" the words in their mind.

THE OGHAM

The Ogham language became the first system of music notation so everyone could read and repeat a harmony.

The Bressay inscription found in the early 19th century below ground-level near St Mary's Church in Shetland shows an early example of music scoring because three of the strokes are identical with three musical signs.

Hecataeus of Miletus (c.550-c.490) is a Greek geographer and researcher and is the first who mentions the Celt, and he describes the Celts of Ireland five hundred years before Christ as singing songs in praise of Apollo and playing melodiously on the harp[9].

This means that the pre-Christian inhabitants of Ireland had the use of letters, the Ogham scale, and the Ogham music showed the fingering for the Irish harp instead of the pitch of notes. Each of the original Ogham feda corresponds to one of the twenty strings of the Irish harp.

Dubhaltach MacFhirbhisigh (1643 – 1671) is an Irish scribe, translator, historian and genealogist who wrote *"The Great Book of Irish Genealogies"* and cited the three great Tuatha de Danann musicians as Ceol (music), Bind (sweet) and Tetbind (sweet-string), while the chief harper was named Uathne (harmony).

---

[9] Even though it was permissible to record secular or popular music, originally it was forbidden to write down Druid sacred or holy music just as sacred doctrine could only be spoken and not written.

THE OGHAM

Thomas Davis (1814 –1845) who organised the Young Ireland movement wrote that "*No enemy speaks slightingly of Irish Music, and no friend need fear to boast of it. It is without a rival Its antique war-tunes, such as those of O'Byrne, O'Donnell, MacAlistrum and Brian Boru, stream and crash upon the ear like the warriors of a hundred glens meeting; and you are borne with them to battle, and they and you charge and struggle amid cries and battle-axes and stinging arrows. Did ever a wail make man's marrow quiver and fill his nostrils with the breath of the grave, like the ululu of the North or the wirrasthrue of Munster?*"

Dr. W. H. Cummings wrote: "*I believe the Irish had the diatonic scale as we have it to-day. It was the advent of the Church scales which supplanted that beautiful scale.*"

Father H Bewerunge the Professor of Ecclesiastical Chant in Maynooth College in 1890 says "*The Irish melodies belong to a stage of musical development very much anterior to that of Gregorian chant. Being based fundamentally on a pentatonic scale, they reach back to a period altogether previous to the dawn of musical history.*"

Ogham Magic

With such a rich trove of stories, traditional spiritual and medicinal uses and energy to draw on for each feda, it makes sense to use your knowledge of the Ogham in magic to enhance your daily life. Just look through the list of meanings assigned to each feda to choose which is most appropriate and then use that feda to call that energy to you.

The Ogham can perform sympathetic magic, with the Ogham letter carved into an amulet or decoration to invite the properties of that sign. For example if you wished to make a fresh start you may choose to use Beith meaning "*New beginnings; changes; purification*" and perhaps Coll meaning "*Creative energies for work or projects*".

Other ways to use the Ogham for magic include drawing these symbols in the air, as you meditate on your intent. For example, you can draw the Ogham symbol for Beith if you wish to make a new start. Visualise the power attributed to that symbol, coming to your desire, as you draw the symbol.

Alternatively, you could carve the symbols on an amulet to carry with you and remind you of your project. Dedicate your amulet during a time of special power, like a Full Moon or festival, or at a New Moon so you can grow your magic wish as the moon grows.

THE OGHAM

Another way to use these symbols is to carve the appropriate symbol onto a candle to ritually dedicate your wish. Choose a candle of an appropriate colour and dress your candle with appropriate oils for your wish. When the time is right, light your candle and meditate on your desire, calling power to your wish as you meditate.

You could also use the symbols to empower the paper on which you write your wishes.

You are only limited by your imagination.

THE AICME BEITH (the B Group)

BEITH (Birch): New beginnings; changes; purification. Your growth is encouraged by personal changes or challenges.
Tarot equivalent: The Star
Physical:

> Rid yourself of negativity, unhelpful influences and bad thoughts for a new, fresh start.

Mental:

> Concentrate on your desire, hold the image of the result you want in your mind.

Spiritual:

> For a new beginning focus on the best outcome free from distractions and obstructions.

THE OGHAM

LUIS (Rowan): Taking control of your life, or a warning to protect yourself against control by others
Tarot equivalent: The Hierophant
Physical:
> Keep your senses about you to distinguish good from bad, and harm from help.

Mental:
> Do not be swayed, tricked or beguiled. Keep your wits about you.

Spiritual:
> Your strength will turn away anything that threatens your purpose and your serenity. Do not fear.

FEARN (Alder): Help in making choices. Spiritual guidance and protection[10].
Tarot equivalent: Strength
Physical:
> Be aware of uniqueness in self and others. If possible salute what you see in another.

Mental:
> You will utilize something you previously overlooked. Oracular skills are not easy to acknowledge. The mind can be unwilling to deal with the intuitive.

Spiritual:
> You offer spiritual aid and protection in a dispute. Let your intuition guide you.

---

[10] Fearn means *"a shield"* and can defend you against the effects of negative emotions

THE OGHAM

SAILLE (Willow): Gaining balance in your life

Tarot equivalent: The Moon

Physical:

> A comfortable relationship to the material world is full of lessons and cycles of changing values. Change is necessary for growth, and values are no exception.

Mental:

> To gain understanding of a particular concept, a steady accumulation of facts is the foundation that brings understanding. All cannot be learned in one lesson. Repetition is the key.

Spiritual:

> This is a time to take it easy rather than full speed ahead. Learn to play with the cyclical nature of life.

NUIN (Ash): Locked into a chain of events

Tarot equivalent: The World

Physical:

> Know that you and the world are interconnected. Be aware of the wider effect of your actions.

Mental:

> Your problems or questions are not yours alone. Look in the wider context and ask opinions.

Spiritual:

> Endeavour to become aware that all things are connected. Balance your need with the Earth's.

THE OGHAM

THE AICME HUATHA (the H Group)

HUATHA (Hawthorn): Being held back for a period of time
Tarot equivalent: Judgement
Physical:

> Work on your physical condition. You can improve your body with diet and exercise. A healthy body encourages a healthy mind.

Mental:

> Open your mind to recognize self-imposed thickets of ignorance and false facts. Free your thoughts and cleanse your mind.

Spiritual:

> However heated the problem is that you face, your spirit will create new and unexpected strengths to handle any challenge.

DUIR (Oak): Security, strength
Tarot equivalent: The Emperor
Physical:

> A hands-on approach will nurture the skills you wish to have. Step through the door, you learn by doing.

Mental:

> You have accumulated acorns of wisdom, the time to share your wisdom is here.

Spiritual:

> You as a teacher or student must be tough and resilient despite life's unpredictability. Welcome the lightning as the Oak does.

THE OGHAM

TINNE (Holly): Energy and guidance for problems to come
Tarot equivalent: The Chariot
Physical:
> Challenges will be overcome with unity and
> concerted effort. Ensure the cause is just.

Mental:
> Every craft master trains and retrains until what they
> do is instinctive, so you must train and learn daily.

Spiritual:
> Cultivate dynamic and instinctive intuition to respond
> to fast moving situations and accept the reality of
> here and now. Ensure the ability of slipping in and
> out of a great variety of behaviour styles, to be able
> to respond to the environment at hand.

COLL (Hazel): Creative energies for work or projects
Tarot equivalent: The High Priestess
Physical:
> Your skill in poetry, divination and meditation allows
> you to inspire others to increase their capacity in
> these arts. Example is the best teacher.

Mental:
> Allow the promptings of your intuition to bring ideas
> to the surface. Become a catalyst with those ideas.

Spiritual:
> Follow your intuition to the source, you will be
> rewarded with wisdom and your soul will sing.

THE OGHAM

QWERT (Apple): A choice must be made
Tarot equivalent: The Empress
Physical:
>Making a choice is not easy, but it is necessary. Stop procrastinating, you will end up with nothing or an unsatisfying taste from each choice.

Mental:
>Many paths of learning are open so choose one. It is better to be master of one than an expert of none.

Spiritual:
>In your journey choose one path to complete. When you do this, the others will follow.

THE AICME MUIN (the M Group)

MUIN (Vine): Inner development occurring, but do take time for relaxation.
Tarot equivalent: The Lovers
Physical:
>Take time to unwind. If you then sense at a deep level that you must act in a certain way to deal with an issue, follow your intuition and do it.

Mental:
>Trust your senses to speed development of your intuition instead of only relying on reason.

Spiritual:
>Open your inner self so it may harvest and gather all signs and omens that it is capable of understanding. Allow yourself this blessing.

THE OGHAM

GORT (Ivy): Take time to soul-search to avoid a wrong decision.
Tarot equivalent: Justice
Physical:
> Link with others. This is not the time to be alone.

Mental:
> Recognize group unconscious has an influence on you, absorb, go inward to learn more about the self.

Spiritual:
> Enter the group mind with joy, assist others in their spiritual journey as they assist in yours. We all are intertwined as the ivy; their success is yours just as your success is theirs.

NGETAL (Reed): Upsets or surprises
Tarot equivalent: Wheel of Fortune
Physical:
> You are able to find order where others find only chaos. Put this valuable skill to work. Take charge.

Mental:
> Your results are as true and sure as your intentions. Keep your target in sight. Do not be distracted.

Spiritual:
> Your journey has begun. Surprises and upsets are to be expected. The skills you develop to overcome these troubles are as valuable as the trip itself.

THE OGHAM

STRAIF (Blackthorn): Resentment; confusion; refusing to see the truth

Tarot equivalent: Temperance

Physical:

> Unexpected change, plans altered or ruined. Events take over forcing you down the unavoidable path. Take courage, issues must be faced, decisions are unavoidable.

Mental:

> Your negative view, clinging to old ways and facing challenges with anger and stubbornness will only make it worse and hurt you more. Accept changes and move on.

Spiritual:

> Realize you and your life have changed radically, enter reborn.

RUIS (Elder): End of a cycle or problem

Tarot equivalent: The Hanged Man

Physical:

> Though one aspect of your life is over, another begins anew.

Mental:

> Changes from the old will bring creativity, to usher in new ideas and thoughts.

Spiritual:

> Links are continually being forged as new phases of life and experience repeat in different forms that lead to renewal.

THE OGHAM

THE AICME AILIM (the A Group)

AILIM (Pine or Silver Fir): Learn from past mistakes. Take care in making choices. Look to past experience for solutions to current problems and to understand the future.
Tarot equivalent: The Devil
Physical:
> You have the perception to see and to understand what is coming. Take the long view to see the future.

Mental:
> Receive from the past and present strength and healing from which to draw insight and knowledge for your future.

Spiritual:
> Be aware of your progress on your spiritual voyage.

OHN (Furze): Discovery of information that could change your life. Continuing towards a goal. Sharing with others.
Tarot equivalent: The Sun
Physical:
> Your search is over. What you seek shall be found. Continue on towards your goal.

Mental:
> Share the knowledge you have gathered, as the bee shares pollen and nectar gathered from the furze.

Spiritual:
> There is an abundance of blessings in your spiritual voyage, do not stockpile and hoard. Share with others, you will be rewarded.

THE OGHAM

UR (Heather): Healing and development on the spiritual level. A time of healing and respite.
Tarot equivalent: The Fool
Physical:
> Listen to your body's messages. Now is the time for healing.

Mental:
> Do not stress. Go inward for healing and respite. This issue can wait.

Spiritual:
> Integrate inner with self to heal and be whole, to build the foundation for what is coming.

EADHA (Aspen or White Poplar): Problems, doubts, fears, misunderstandings. Facing challenges with determination.
Tarot equivalent: The Falling Tower
Physical:
> Whatever challenge you now face, you will endure and conquer. You can bend and not break.

Mental:
> Shield your thoughts from the fears and doubts about the odds you must overcome. A positive attitude will prevail.

Spiritual:
> Do not give in to worldly pressure, know that help is always on hand when you need it.

THE OGHAM

IOHO (Yew): Complete change in life-direction or attitude. Letting go. Accepting change.
Tarot equivalent: Death
Physical:

Something held for many years must be passed on, let go. It serves you no longer.

Mental:

The knowledge that nothing lasts forever will bring ease at this time.

Spiritual:

Changes are coming to you, you have a tendency to try and hang on, let go and experience change as an ally and not an enemy.

THE FORFEDA

CHELWYDD (Mistletoe): Wisdom gained by seeing past illusions
Tarot equivalent: The Hermit
Physical:

You could be part of a resolution of conflict.

Mental:

Misunderstandings can be ironed out if all parties will meet and honestly work together.

Spiritual:

Try to hold the energy of judgement, of life aligned to values that are above reproach. We teach others best by example.

THE OGHAM

OIR (Spindle): Sudden positive change or sudden revelations. Finish obligations and tasks or your life cannot move forward. Commitment. honour and inner peace. Wealth or inspired knowledge. Gold.

Tarot equivalent: Six of Wands

Physical:

>Fulfil your obligations, not for reward but because it is right for you to do, honour demands it and the greatest happiness will be yours.

Mental:

>Sudden realization gives you the right and obligation to question authority.

Spiritual:

>Develop your consciousness of the right relationship with others in the community and tribe.

UILLEAND (Honeysuckle): Proceed with caution; know what is real and what is false especially when you seek pleasure.

Tarot equivalent: *Seven of Swords*

Physical:

>Pursue your desires, allow yourself to experience pleasure. We learn by being happy, not by abstinence from what we enjoy.

Mental:

>Hidden secrets you pursue are not as unfathomable as you believe. They are lost in background noises. Put aside distraction to find what you seek.

Spiritual:

>Remain true to your beliefs and principles. Follow the honeysuckle in safety and joy.

THE OGHAM

IPHIN (Gooseberry): Sweetness of life, divine influences, happy memories
Tarot equivalent: Six of Cups
Physical:
> Good opportunity for enrichment or improvement in living conditions.

Mental:
> Creativity can be released as you focus on a happy series of events which bring pleasant memories.

Spiritual:
> Transform yourself by remembering your uniqueness, just as the taste of ripe gooseberry is unusual but pleasant.

EAMANCHOLL (Beech): New experiences and information is coming. Be alert for a new opportunity. Let go of fixed ideas. Learn from the past. Hidden depths, travel, journey.
Tarot equivalent: *Four of Cups*
Physical:
> Reviving memories will bring understanding that is needed. Do not neglect the past; it is rich in experience.

Mental:
> Heed the echoes in your mind; memories will give wisdom to make the changes necessary.

Spiritual:
> Do not discount the past as old fashioned, you have paid a price for experience. Remember, respect and listen to the inner voices and you will not go wrong.

Ogham Divination

Although there is evidence that the ancients used the Ogham for divination[11], it is more likely that the ancient singers of the Ogham would go sit peacefully in a grove of trees to listen for messages and wisdom.

Today we prefer quicker ways to seek answers to current questions or to predict the future. As well as performing magic, you can use the meanings given in the Magic section for divination and make a deck of cards with the symbols or use flat sticks or stones with the symbol painted, carved or engraved on one side.

The usual Ogham set consists of 25 wooden sticks, each carved with its own feda to represent a spiritual meaning.

---

[11] The Macogam or Boy Ogham is a technique for divining the sex of an unborn child. The name of the pregnant woman "*is divided there unless she bear a child previously. If however she bear a child previously, it is the child's name that is divided there; and if there be a letter over, it is a boy. If it be an even number, it would be a daughter that will be born of that pregnancy.*" This seems that a name with an odd number of letters foretells a boy, an even number a girl.

THE OGHAM

Divination by using Ogham feda is mentioned in Tochmarc Étaíne[12], a tale in the Irish Mythological Cycle. In the story, the Druid Dalan cut four wands of yew on which he cut three feda on each wand, and with them he found the "*eochra ecsi (keys of divination/knowledge)*" with which he was able to discover that Etaine had been taken to the Sidhe-mound of Breg Leith, where Midir lived.

Omen sticks are called coelbreni in some areas, and eochra ecsi in other places. In early Ireland, the omen sticks are known as fidlanna. Rowan is a good wood to make omen sticks because wands made from the rowan are used for knowledge, locating metal and general divination.

The omen sticks are trusted servants. The Senchus Mor[13] describes a judgement used to find a murderer or a thief, which is called crannchur or casting the woods.

It is possible that this Druid method of divination is where our child's game of *"Pick Up Sticks"* originated.

---

[12] Tochmarc Étaíne meaning "*The Wooing of Étaín*" is an early text of the Irish Mythological Cycle partially preserved in the manuscript known as the Lebor na hUidre (1106AD), and completely preserved in the Yellow Book of Lecan (1401AD), but written in language believed to date to the 8th or 9th century.

[13] In the year 438AD Laegaire, the king of Ireland, appointed a committee of nine learned and eminent persons including himself and St. Patrick to revise the old Irish laws. At the end of three years these nine produced a new legal code, the Senchus Mor, from which everything that clashed with Christian doctrine was excluded.

THE OGHAM

Casting the omen sticks

Basic Casting (1 stick):
Shuffle the sticks lightly in a carrying bag. Reach into the bag and pull out a single stick to answer immediate enquiries, or to use as a talisman for that day.

Awen Casting or "*Ray of Light*" spread (3 sticks):
Shuffle the sticks lightly. Reach into the bag and pull one stick and place to the left to represent your past. Next, pull out another stick and place this to your right to represent your future. Lastly, pull one stick and place in the middle. This stick represents the "*in between*" or the Now and ideally this is where we want to be. When you look on the past and learn from it, you will gain the strength and insight to face the future. Alternate ways to use the Awen Casting is if you have questions about the three worlds of land, sea and sky[14] or the three states of physical, mental and spiritual.

Celtic Cross (Brigid's Cross) (5 sticks):
This is like the Awen layout but the two sticks placed on either side of the middle stick represent masculine and feminine forces, and those above and below respectively represent our past and future. The stick on the left side represents our feminine side; that which supports us and from where we draw energy. The stick on the right symbolises our masculine side; what needs our attention and where we should place our energy and best efforts.

---

[14] See Appendix 1:The Celtic Worlds

THE OGHAM

Circle casting (5 sticks):

$$5$$
$$3 \quad 4$$
$$1 \quad 2$$

- Stick 1 represents the querant, situation or problem.
- Stick 2 represents the cause of the problem; the reason for the reading or even another angle on the question asked.
- Stick 3 represents outside factors or influences to be considered.
- Stick 4 represents comments and advice to assist the querant with the problem.
- Stick 5 represents the outcome or end result.

Row casting (7 sticks):

$$6 \quad 5 \quad 4 \quad 3 \quad 2 \quad 1$$
$$7$$

- Sticks 1 and 2 represent the problem.
- Sticks 3 and 4 are the outside factors influencing the situation.
- Sticks 5 & 6 are your answer.
- Stick 7 is the final outcome which will eventuate from the solution offered.

Casting Seven Omen Sticks

Another way to use the Ogham for divination is to first concentrate on your question, as you choose seven sticks without looking. Then toss your chosen sticks on the ground or floor in front of you. The closest sticks are the present, the sticks that are further away show the future. Any sticks that touch or overlap have a direct influence on each other, and increase the individual meaning of that stick.

 # The Ogham Astrology

Celtic astrology is part of the Celtic craft of divination, one of the 36 crafts which are recognized in the old interlocking system of tribal beliefs. As the time of our birth is pivotal to the formation of our personality and behaviour we can associate the likeness and personality of trees to our own human nature, gathering insight and clarity into who we are.

The Celtic calendar is lunar and so divides into thirteen lunar months. Thirteen of the trees used in the tree alphabet that symbolise the characteristics of people born during that time make up this astrology.

Celtic Astrology at a glance:

Period	Ogham	English
24 December to 20 January	Beith	Birch
21 January to 17 February	Luis	Rowan
18 February to 17 March	Nuin	Ash
18 March to 14 April	Fearn	Alder
15 April to 12 May	Saille	Willow
13 May to 9 June	Huatha	Hawthorn
10 June to 7 July	Duir	Oak
8 July to 4 August	Tinne	Holly
5 August to 1 September	Coll	Hazel
2 to 29 September	Muin	Vine
30 September to 27 October	Gort	Ivy
28 October to 24 November	Ngetal	Reed
25 November to 23 December	Ruis	Elder

THE OGHAM

BEITH (Birch): The Achiever
24 December [an Dubhlachd] to 20 January [am Faoilleach]

Planet of Influence: The Sun
Tarot Equivalent: The Star
Traditional Zodiac Association: Capricorn
Animal Totem: White Stag
Personality: Renewal

The Birch represents renewal and rebirth as it is the first tree in leaf after winter. You always reach for more, seeking bigger horizons and higher aspirations because your time of birth is the darkest time in the Northern hemisphere, so you always seek the light.

Birch people are tolerant, tough and resilient, like the tree but you are also highly driven and can easily become caught up and catch others up in your zeal, drive and ambition. You are a natural leader and cool under pressure.

When you are in touch with your softer side, you bring beauty with you and can brighten a room with your charisma and charm crowds with your quick wit.

Good organisers, leaders and strategists, Birch people are not deterred by misfortune. You have a firm belief in your own ability and believe that patience and hard work will triumph in the end. Although Birch people don't often show affection, you are loyal to your selected friends. You do need a goal in life or you could become depressed and pessimistic.

THE OGHAM

Your totem animal is the white stag which symbolises high ideals and aspirations. The stag brings the qualities of grace, majesty and integrity to remind you of your best qualities. According to Welsh tradition, the stag is one of the five oldest animals in the world, one of the five British totem animals who carries both Merlin and the King of Faery.

The gift, quality or ability for this sign is sensitivity to the otherworld, shape-shifting, journeying, and connecting to the element of Earth. If you are born in this sign you have unwavering inner strength and gladly support those who rely on you. Purity of thought, a knack for realistic evaluation and quiet determination are associated with this tree sign.

You are most compatible with Vines and Willows.

Your Beech friends and family include:

THE OGHAM

LUIS (Rowan): The Thinker
21 January [am Faoilleach] to 17 February [an Gearran]

Planet of Influence: Uranus
Deity: Brigid
Tarot Equivalent: The Hierophant
Traditional Zodiac Association: Aquarius
Animal Totem: Dragon
Personality: Philosopher

Aloof, detached Rowan people are secretly idealistic, progressive thinkers with strong principles who are original thinkers, impatient with restrictions and enjoy change.

You are the philosopher of all the zodiac signs, a keen-minded visionary with high ideals. Your thoughts are original and creative, so unusual and out of the ordinary that other people may misunderstand you.

Beneath a cool exterior you burn with passionate ideals. You have a natural ability to transform situations and people around you, influential in your quiet way and others look to you for your unique perspective. You also have a kind, humanitarian quality that makes you lovable.

Your animal symbol the dragon symbolises inspiration and imagination and Rowans need an outlet for their imagination or they can become restless and quarrelsome.

The Druids believe that the Earth is a dragon so they sited their sacred stone circles on the power nodes to connect us with the Earth's magnetism and healing waters.

THE OGHAM

Ley lines are called dragon lines, so the "*ley of the land*" was about more than the geographical nature of the land and would map how the Universal forces flow through and influence the area, as well as how the area itself interacts with those forces.

Your tree symbol the rowan is a tree of high magic, from which potent charms are made. Rowans are planted near doors and gates to ward off evil and are guard the gateway to the spirit world. The Gaelic word for the rowan is the letter L-Luis, which also means flame, hand, branch, mantle or pure. This can be traced to the Rowan's close association with the goddess Brigid. The Festival of Bride falls on the eve of 1st February, and is the celebration of the fire of illumination, the impulse of inspiration, of healing and creative energy. Brigid is the triple goddess of Fire, Poetry and the Forge. If you are a Rowan you use your intuition and higher understanding to enchant and protect. Quite often you are seen as unusual by others due to your ability to see the future and your unorthodox vision is often called on by others when fresh new perspectives are needed in a project.

You are most compatible with Ivy and Hawthorn people.

Your Rowan friends and family include:

THE OGHAM

NUIN (Ash): The Enchanter
18 February [an Gearran] to 17 March [am Mart]

Planet of Influence: Neptune
Tarot Equivalent: The World
Traditional Zodiac Association: Aquarius and Pisces
Animal Totem: Adder
Personality: Enthusiasm, inquisitiveness and spontaneity

You are a free thinker, imaginative, intuitive and naturally artistic. Quick-witted and gregarious Ash people need to focus or you can become nervous and irritable.

With your lively curiousity and intelligent, persuasive communication style, you love discussing new ideas and projects and although you are quite flexible, you like things to go your way and may be uncooperative, moody and withdrawn if pushed into a corner.

Art, writing, science and spiritual matters are areas that strongly interest you. You are in a constant state of self-renewal and although you rarely place a value on what others think about you, you naturally inspire others and attract friends easily with your lively personality.

You are curious and are always full of questions about how the world and the people around you work. Even if you don't openly ask, you can be sure that you are figuring out the answers in your own mind. You are a natural communicator and can be very persuasive. If you are passionate about a cause you can round up the whole neighbourhood and inspire them with your enthusiasm.

THE OGHAM

Your animal symbol is the Adder, which symbolises healing, transformation and life energy. Welsh bards referred to the Druids as Naddred, or adders, and it is possible that the story of St Patrick ridding Ireland of snakes refers to the Druids. The adder is poisonous and reminds us of the mystery of death and rebirth and of the soul's journey through from this world to the next and back again.

The Ash is a sacred chieftain tree, said to *"court the flash"* as it is prone to lightning strike. Its wood is enchanted and is used to make Druidic wands and spears. You were born knowing of the connection between ourselves, our planet, and our universe. You feel the pain and joys of all living creatures, which makes you compassionate. The gift, quality or ability for your sign is healing and creativity.

Ash people are most compatible with Willows and Reeds.

Your Ash friends and family include:

THE OGHAM

FEARN (Alder): The Trailblazer
18 March [am Mart] to 14 April [an Giblean]

Planet of Influence: Mars
Element: Fire
Rank: Chieftain
Diety: Bran the Blessed, the God of the Spirit World
Tarot Equivalent: Strength
Traditional Zodiac Association: Pisces and Aries
Animal Totem: Fox
Personality: Courage, energy and impetuosity.

Self-reliant Fearns make their own way in the world, love taking risks and work stubbornly. You are a natural-born pathfinder, a mover and shaker and you will blaze a trail with fiery passion, often gaining loyal followers to your cause.

You are charming and gregarious, mingle easily and your self-assurance is infectious so you make many loyal friends through your affectionate and charming nature.

You are very focused and you dislike waste. You have the ability to see through superficialities and you don't suffer fools gladly.

You place high value on your time and are motivated by action and results. You have a knack for story-telling and every experience is fodder for your tales. You can be tender-hearted but don't show your soft side often, you prefer laughing and cracking jokes.

THE OGHAM

The animal totem for Fearn is fox, which symbolises skill in diplomacy. Although you have tremendous courage and personal power to win disputes, you do need to study fox energy because you may waste energy trying to win unwinnable disputes. Fox energy is cunning and knows how to work a room with sexy humour. When you use guile, enthusiasm and intelligence the fox is an unstoppable force.

While Fearn is the Gaelic word for the Alder tree, it can also mean a shield offering protection against negative emotions. Alder is widely used for making milk pails to protect the milk from souring. It is also one of the nine sacred woods used to kindle the Beltaine fire, although it is a poor fuel tree giving off little more than smouldering smoke. However, it does give one of the finest grades of charcoal.

Fearns are most compatible with those born in Hawthorn, Oak and Birch.

Your Fearn friends and family include:

THE OGHAM

SAILLE (Willow): The Observer
15 April [an Giblean] to 12 May [an Ceitean]

Planet of Influence: Moon
Element: Water
Rank: Chieftain
Tarot Equivalent: The Moon
Traditional Zodiac Association: Aries and Taurus
Animal Totem: Hare
Personality: Emotional and enigmatic

Willow people have excellent memories, and you are both shrewd and practical as well as being intelligent, patient, creative and intuitive.

Your strong will can sometimes be mistaken for stubbornness but you mellow this trait with resourcefulness, quick responses, sudden mood changes and endearing loyalty. You are the one that your friends turn to when they need a shoulder to cry on, honest opinions and solid advice because you are trustworthy, know how to keep a secret and your intuition can spot a liar from a mile away.

You have excellent taste and a flair for classy elegance in fashion and home décor. Willows often surprise even their closest friends with the brilliance of their extraordinary inventions. You have a natural ability to retain knowledge and you often impress your friends with your ability to expound on subjects from memory.

Although you have great potential you do hold yourself back for fear of appearing flamboyant or overindulgent.

THE OGHAM

You have good instincts and react to gut responses rather than intellectual information. You can trust your intuition and pay close attention to your dreams because they will help you navigate through life.

Your tree totem, the Willow, is sacred to the Moon. People born in this time find that the Moon is their planet of influence, and their Tarot equivalent is also the Moon so this triple Moon influence is why Willow people are extremely intuitive, with an inner knowledge that is often beyond rational explanation.

The Willow totem animal is the Hare, which symbolises adaptation and intuition. Those people born in Willow must learn to trust their intuition or they can lose their way and become capricious and irresolute.

Willows are most compatible with the Birch and the Ivy.

Your Willow friends and family include:

THE OGHAM

HUATHA (Hawthorn): The Illusionist
13 May [an Ceitean] to 9 June [an t-Ogmios]

Planet of Influence: Vulcan
Element: Fire
Tarot Equivalent: Judgement
Traditional Zodiac Association: Taurus and Gemini
Animal Totem: Owl
Personality: Naturally charming, articulate and gifted

Hawthorn people are confident and creative. They are mercurial innovators who become easily bored when they don't achieve the stimulation and challenge they seek as quickly as they desire.

You are not always what you appear to be but you are still the best person to manage finances or handle legal matters because you are so clever. If there is a loophole, you have either found it or invented it.

You often give off a different persona than the one inside you and can be changeable, but always return to being charming because you like being liked. You are well-adjusted and can adapt to most life situations which makes you content and gives you the ability to comfort others.

You are naturally curious, with an interest in a broad range of topics. You are an excellent listener and other people know this instinctively. You have a good sense of humour and a clear understanding of irony. You see the big picture and have sharp insight but it is typical of you not to give yourself credit for your observations.

THE OGHAM

Your animal symbol of owl reminds Hawthorn people of your special need to cultivate wisdom and patience. This virtue is so necessary to Hawthorns because your tendency to act impetuously without thinking can ruin your best ideas.

If born under this sign you have an innate understanding of the importance of process and the necessity for change.

Hawthorns are most compatible with Ash and Rowan people.

Your Hawthorn friends and family include:

THE OGHAM

DUIR (Oak): The Stabiliser
10 June [an t-Ogmios] to 7 July [an t-Iuchar]

Planet of Influence: Jupiter
Rank: Chieftain
Element: Fire
Tarot Equivalent: The Emperor
Traditional Zodiac Association: Gemini and Cancer
Animal Totem: Wren
Personality: a natural leader

Oak people are determined, self-motivated, enthusiastic and responsible. You remain calm in a crisis and are not easily swayed by opposition. Although you can be very serious, you are also cheerful and optimistic and do not give up easily.

You have the strength of character and purpose to endure, no matter what challenges. Direct your energies wisely because you have a special strength.

You despise injustice and often become a champion or spokesperson for those who cannot defend themselves. You are likely to be involved with social and community networks. You have a need for structure and will often become a leader at work or in the community to ensure that everything runs well, even though you would secretly rather be a carefree gypsy without heavy responsibilities.

You exude an easy confidence and assume everything will turn out well. You have a deep respect for history and ancestry and you like to impart your knowledge of the past to others.

THE OGHAM

Those born in Oak are likely to live long, full and happy lives. Oak is an important symbol in Druidic lore as it is strong, tall and very long-lived.

Your animal symbol is the wren, the Celtic king of birds, which symbolises wit and subtlety. Those born in this sign need to learn how to temper pride with humour or you may be seen by others as pompous and overbearing.

Oaks are compatible with Ash and Reed people, as well as with Ivy.

Your Oak friends and family include:

THE OGHAM

TINNE (Holly): The Ruler
8 July [an t-Iuchar] to 4 August [an Lunasdal]

Planet of Influence: Earth
Element: Fire
Tarot Equivalent: The Chariot
Traditional Zodiac Association: Cancer and Leo
Animal Totem: Unicorn
Personality: Logical, cautious and efficient.

Hollies are practical and steadfast in life, as well as being protective and supportive of those you care most about. You can also be possessive.

You have a strong connection with the Earth and possess amazing physical strength. Your matter-of-fact solidness and generous spirit are respected and admired by others.

You are comfortable taking on challenges and you overcome obstacles with a skill and tact.

You are competitive and ambitious and can appear arrogant to those who don't know you well enough to know you are confident in your own abilities. Once people get to know you, they'll find you are generous, kind and affectionate.

Because many things come to you easily, you may be tempted to rest on your laurels. You have a lot of talent and confidence, are gregarious and openly charming. You know how to make a grand appearance and do well in leadership positions but you are just as happy to be a follower provided you are recognized for your talents and contribution.

THE OGHAM

Your totem animal the unicorn is perfection, promising both purity and strength. Hollies should learn not to demand perfection of themselves or they may lose both direction and confidence.

Hollies are most compatible with Ash and Elder.

Your Holly friends and family include:

THE OGHAM

COLL (Hazel): The Knower
5 August [an Lunasdal] to 1 September [an t-Sultainn]

Planet of Influence: Mercury
Tarot Equivalent: High Priestess
Traditional Zodiac Association: Leo and Virgo
Animal Totem: Salmon
Personality: Organised and efficient

Hazel people are lively intellectuals who are both perceptive and artistic. You are smart, well-informed and have the ability to retain information which means you can accurately recall and explain subjects which means you excel in the classroom. Because of your knowledge base and eye for detail, you usually know the right course of action to take but sometimes your need for order and control can lead you to compulsive behaviour if left unchecked.

You have a knack for numbers, science and things that utilise your analytical skills. You like rules, but you prefer to be the person making them rather than playing by them. You do need to express your creativity or you can become morbid and introspective. Your unique view of the world, your imagination and intelligence could lead you to radical paths and your idealism helps you to teach others well. You need quiet time to allow your ideas to develop into all they can be.

To the Celts, your totem animal salmon is the eldest and wisest animal symbolising inspiration and your tree the hazel is considered a container of ancient knowledge.

THE OGHAM

Eating hazel nuts induces visions, heightened awareness and can lead to epiphanies. Fionn Mac Cumhail gained the wisdom of the universe by contact with the essence of the hazel nut, when he sucked his finger which he burned cooking a salmon that ate hazel nuts. The hazel nut has proven itself to be a brain food because the hazel has double the protein and good fats than eggs, making hazel natural nourishment for brain function.

When you are stuck creatively call on the energy of the hazel tree, eat a few hazelnuts, or wear a necklace of hazel nuts. Just make sure you pick your hazel nuts after they have fallen from the tree because it is considered bad form to pick them unripe off the branches.

Hazels are most compatible with Hawthorn and Rowan.

Your Hazel friends and family include:

THE OGHAM

MUIN (Vine): The Equaliser
2 September [an t-Sultainn] and 29 September

Planet of Influence: Venus
Element: Water
Tarot Equivalent: The Lovers
Traditional Zodiac Association: Virgo and Libra
Animal Totem: Swan
Personality: Charm, elegance and balance

You were born within the period of autumnal equinox, a time of balance which gives you the ability to restore balance to all situations. Despite this ability, inside you can be unpredictable and indecisive and this trait helps you see both sides of every story so it is hard for you to pick sides.

You are only really sure about the finer things in life like food, wine, music and art. You are a connoisseur with distinctive taste.

Luxury agrees with you and you have the ability to turn drab into dazzling. You are charming and elegant and a natural socializer. Vine people are instinctive and amazingly perceptive but you need to overcome your tendency to procrastinate or you could become lost in worry and negativity.

The animal totem for this time is the swan, which symbolises grace and beauty. Vine people do set high personal standards for themselves, and unfortunately sometimes for others as well.

THE OGHAM

You are a natural aristocrat and very discriminating due to your attention to detail and refined taste, and while you appear cool and detached on the surface you are a secret romantic.

The vine needs loving care to bear fruit in the cool Celtic climates and so became a symbol of hidden knowledge and spiritual initiation.

Vines are compatible with Willow and Hazel.

Your Vine friends and family include:

THE OGHAM

GORT (Ivy): The Survivor
30 September [an t-Suiltainn] to 27 October [an Damhair]

Planet of Influence: Persephone
Element: Earth
Tarot Equivalent: Justice
Traditional Zodiac Association: Libra and Scorpio
Animal Totem: Butterfly
Personality: Gentle dreamer, always in motion

You are a true *"social butterfly"* flitting from party to party and always in contact with loved ones.

Butterflies are gentle souls who can't be tied down for very long, love to dream, express new ideas and talk about their plans with all their friends. Butterflies are the people who brighten up any dark day with their cheer and magnetically bright personalities. They are naturally empathetic, and would never intentionally harm anyone. Rather, they make easy friends, and like to see others uplifted.

Butterflies bring a sense of wonder and youth to our world. Keep these people around you to remind you of how truly good life can be. They dislike antagonising other people, and are extremely sociable and happy creatures. Their intrinsic good nature helps them to make friends easily.

Even though they can be cautious and deliberate over decisions, they are not weak and take on big responsibilities with cheerful optimism. If you are born under this sign your abilities further your personal goals and your personal causes. Be sure to use this talent productively.

THE OGHAM

Among other cherished qualities of this sign, the most prized is your ability to overcome all odds. You have a sharp intellect, but more obvious is your compassion and loyalty to others. You have a giving nature, and are always there to lend a helping hand. You were born at the time of the waning sun so life can be difficult for you at times by putting obstacles in your way, but you endure troubling times with silent perseverance and grace.

Ivy signs have a tendency to be deeply spiritual and cling to a deep-rooted faith that sees them through adversity. You are softly-spoken and you have a keen wit. You are charming, charismatic and can hold your own in most social settings.

The butterfly animal symbol symbolises Faerie faith, and reminds those born in this time to live their own lives and not to become too touched by the problems of others. Ivy people can become very disappointed and disillusioned by their friends, when their expectations are not met. Ivy people are always in motion, like their symbol the butterfly.

Ivy is most compatible with Oak and Ash.

Your Ivy friends and family include:

THE OGHAM

NGETAL (the Reed): The Inquisitor
28 October [an Damhair] to 24 November [an t-Samhainn]

Planet of Influence: Pluto
Element: Air
Tarot Equivalent: Wheel of Fortune
Traditional Zodiac Association: Scorpio and Sagittarius
Animal Totem: Dog
Personality: Pride and independence

You are the secret keeper of the Celtic tree zodiac signs, because you like to know the truth. You dig deep until you find the real meaning of things and can find the truth hidden beneath layers of distraction. You collect gossip, scandal, legend and lore which makes you an excellent writer, historian, journalist, detective or archaeologist.

People interest you which is lucky because people love talking to you and will often share their innermost secrets. You have a strong sense of truth and honour but need to unite a sense of purpose with your strong will or you can become self-destructive.

Reed people are proud, fiercely independent and will rarely compromise. Your complex personality traits include tenacity and apparent fearlessness, and you can show great strength of character. You will go to great lengths to make sure your point is made and fully understood.

You have an innate belief in your own destiny, and will master challenges through sheer determination.

THE OGHAM

If you are born under this sign you have secret strengths, as well as secret motivations. Use your detective abilities wisely. Reed people are often scholars and despite their interest in people, are often loners. You will always know where you stand with a Reed person and they will unite with you and fiercely defend you for as long as you share their beliefs with honour.

The dog or hound is one of the Celt's totem animals; a blend of loyal servant, guardian of the house and fierce battle companion. Hound was a title of honour for Celtic chieftains as the dog symbolised enduring loyalty. In the Gaelic the word for dog is "*cu*", and name of the greatest hero of Ulster, Cuchulain, actually means hound of Culain or hound of the king. The hound is particularly sacred to the Triple Goddess of the Celts, for the hound is the animal chosen to guard her Mysteries. For this reason, dogs are often featured on Celtic knotwork.

Reed people are compatible with other Reeds, Ash or Oaks.

Your Reed friends and family include:

THE OGHAM

RUIS (Elder): The Seeker
25 November [an t-Samhainn] to
23 December [an Dubhlachd]

Planet of Influence: Saturn
Element: Earth
Tarot Equivalent: The Hanged Man
Traditional Zodiac Association: Sagittarius and Capricorn
Animal Totem: Raven
Personality: Energetic and outspoken, the wild child

Elder people are energetic, self-sufficient, impetuous and outspoken and are the wild ones of the Celtic zodiac. You prefer change to routine and refuse to be pressured by other people's desires. You need constant challenge on every level; intellectually, emotionally, spiritually and physically.

Those born under this sign are able to live and prosper under any conditions. You live many lives during your time here and will carry memories into every venture.

You are a gypsy and a student gathering experience and knowledge to eventually become a great teacher. You tend to be freedom-loving, the wild one of the zodiac.

In younger years you may have lived life in the fast lane, perhaps even identified as a thrill seeker. Other people may see you as an outsider because you can be withdrawn, despite your extrovert tendencies, and are deeply thoughtful with a philosophical bent.

You also tend to be very considerate of others and genuinely strive to be helpful although this can go awry due to your brutal honesty.

Your animal totem symbolises healing and protection. Elders should look to their totem raven to learn to how to use change as a positive force in their lives, or they can become reckless and confused.

Elders are most compatible with Alders and Hollies.

Your Elder friends and family include:

THE OGHAM

Appendix 1: THE CELTIC WORLD

The Celtic reverence for trees is part of a vast interlocking spiritual belief system, a spiral of life that connects all life who inhabit sea, land and sky. We humans are land based, but we are connected to and influenced by what happens in sea and sky and trees connect the three realms.

MAG MOR

The Realm of Sky is Above, the Otherworld called Magh Mor or Great Plain. This is the future where inspiration, creativity and wisdom live. The realm of sky is the pathway of the sun, of the moon, the planets and stars, as well as the wind and the weather. Within this realm we will find:

- **Magh Findargat** or the Plain of Silver which grants light and hope,
- **Magh Imchiunn** or the Plain of Kindness which grants kindness and tenderness,
- **Magh Argetnel** or the Plain of Clouds which contains the power of weather and reveals mysteries,
- **Magh Mel** or the Plain of Triumph which grants creativity and inspiration,
- **Magh Ildathach** or the Plain of Many Colours which grants sight and sense,
- **Magh Airthech** or the Plain of Bounty which grants riches,
- **Magh Longanaidh** or the Plain of Miracles which grants miracles and finally
- **Magh Sen** or the Plain of Ages which grants new beginnings and wisdom.

THE OGHAM

MIDE

Our human world occupies the Realm of Land, Mide, or Middle World, the land of the present. This is the realm of humans, plants and animals as well as the deities who are responsible for nature and humans, and the five cardinal directions:

- **East** grants prosperity and change,
- **South** grants poetry and music,
- **West**-grants knowledge,
- **North** grants strength and resolve and the
- **Centre** grants sovereignty and kingship.

TIR ANDOMAIN

The Realm of Sea is the Underworld, Tir Andomain, where the ancestors and the deities responsible for the cycle of life, death and rebirth live. This is the realm of the past where you will find:

- **Tir na mBeo** or the Land of Eternal Life governing eternity and history,
- **Tir na mBan** or the Land of Women governing beauty and pleasure,
- **Tir fo Thuinn** or the Land under the Sea governing fear and attitude, and
- **Tir na n'Og** or the Land of the Young governing needs and rejuvenation.

Human heroes or their champions can journey between the three worlds because caves, burial mounds, wells and springs provide secret entries for us to the underworld, while trees in our world link all three realms with their roots deep in the underworld and their branches in the sky.

THE OGHAM

The three realms can be called upon to take oaths, to call for blessings and to offer good wishes:

> *"Power of sea be thine,*
> *Power of land be thine,*
> *Power of heaven*
>
> *Goodness of sea be thine,*
> *Goodness of land be thine,*
> *Goodness of heaven"*

The three realms offer a wholeness, balance and order to mortal man living in a chaotic land at the mercy of wind, weather and politics. By using the three realms in oaths, charms and blessings we can restore balance and order to our own world.

THE OGHAM

Appendix 2: OGHAM ETYMOLOGY & VARIATIONS

 The etymology of the word Ogham is unclear. One possible origin is from the Irish word og-úaim which means point-seam and refers to the seam made by the point of a sharp weapon, but it is more likely to be named for the Irish god, Ogma, a member of the Tuatha Dé Danann[15] who is the god of speech, language, eloquence and learning.

There are many variations to the Ogham probably because the original Ogham was not a written language, even though there are 400 orthodox inscriptions of personal names on stone monuments through Ireland and Wales.

Three different variations of early word Oghams known today are:
1. the Briatharogam Morainn mac Moin,
2. the Briatharogam Maic ind Oc, and the
3. Briatharogam Cu Culainn.

The first two come from the Ogham Tract which lists some 100 modes of writing Ogham while the Cu Culainn version is known from 16th and 17th century manuscripts. In later centuries when the Ogham was no longer a practical alphabet, it was still used as a foundation for grammar and to set the rules of poetry by Gaelic scholars and poets. Until recently the Latin alphabet in Gaelic was taught using letter names borrowed from the Ogham.

---

[15] The Tuatha Dé Danann are a supernatural race and the main deities of pre-Christian Gaelic Ireland. Although they dwell in the Otherworld they interact with humans and our human world.

THE OGHAM

There are also many different beliefs as to why the Ogham was created. One school of thought is that the Ogham is like an ancient version of the 1940's Enigma cipher, a cryptic alphabet to provide a secret means of communication for political, military or religious reasons which could not be understood by the Roman invaders. This is credible when you look at some of the Ogham varieties, like:

- **Cend a muine**[16]: Writing a letter to stand in for the whole letter name at the beginning of a word when possible e.g., to write simply CLE for ceirtle[17].

- **Cend fo muine**[18]: This is the opposite of Cend a muine, where the letter stands in for the name at the end of a word e.g. MAELR for Maelruis[19].

- **Ogam Dedanach**[20]: The last letter of the name of the letter is written instead of the letter i.e. E for B, S for L, N for F, L for S, N for N and so on.

- **Cend ar Nuaill**[21]: The last letter of every group is written for the first letter, and the first letter of every group for the last letter, i.e. N for B, and B for N, and every letter for its fellow in the whole group, i.e. L for S and S for L.

---

[16] Head in bush
[17] A ceirtle is a ball of yarn
[18] Head under bush
[19] Saint Máel Ruain who died in 792AD was founder and abbot-bishop of the monastery of Tallaght in Dublin and was a leader of the monastic faction that has become known as the Culdees.
[20] Final Ogham
[21] Head on Proscription

THE OGHAM

Some forms of Ogham contain extra groups or syllables, possibly for students to learn as part of their grammatical training:

- **Foraicimib 7 Deachaib**: Bacht, lact, fect, sect, nect; huath, drong, tect, caect, quiar; maei, gaeth, ngael, strmrect, rect; ai, ong, ur, eng, ing.

Some appear to be useful for music:

- **Aradach Fionn**[22]: Each letter has its own vertical stemline which can be used as musical notation.

While other variations use decorative dots, V or X shapes, wavy lines, wheels, circles and squares:

- **Ogam Bricrenn**[23] One dot for B, two dots for L, three dots for F and so on right up to twenty dots for I. This Ogham was used to record the thoughts of a poet who bemoaned his lack of an appetizing drink.

  'Mountain water does not satisfy me
  A boon that makes me pull a wry face
  Drink of a brown deer that bellows
  Maybe it enjoys it, but I do not'

- **Ogam Erimon**[24]: Has angles or 'V' shapes against the stemline for the aicme, from one to five as needed.

---

[22] Fionn's Ladder

[23] This alphabet is named after Briciu, the satirical poet who was famous for his mischievous tongue and skill in inciting trouble in the court of the Ulster King Conchubar Mac Neasa

[24] Erimon was the first king to rule all of Ireland.

THE OGHAM

- **Ogam Snaithi Snimach**[25]: Instead of strokes there are 'X's, with one laid on top of another from one to five.

- **Nathair fria Fraech**[26]: A wavy line weaves above and below the letters like a snake.

- **Rothogam Roigni Roscadhaig**[27]: This Ogham looks like a wooden wheel or shield, with the letter c repeated to look like bosses or pegs.

- **Fege[28] Find/Fionn's[29] Window**: The letters are arranged in a series of circles.

- **Traig Sruth Ferchertne[30]**: The letters are arranged in a series of squares.

The Ogham scholar R.A.S. Macalister[31] thinks that Ogham was first invented around 600BC by Druids and used as a secret system of hand signals.

---

[25] Ogham of Interwoven Thread
[26] Ogham of Snake through Heather
[27] Wheel Ogham of Roigne Roscadach means *"Choicest Rhetoric"*
[28] The word fege means a ridgepole used to hold up a house
[29] Named for the great Gaelic warrior Fionn mac Cumhaill
[30] Ferchertne was an ancient Irish poet whose skill was so great that it was said that *'the lakes and rivers drain before him when he satirises, and they rise up when he praises them'*.
[31] Robert Alexander Stewart Macalister (8 July 1870 – 26 April 1950) was an Irish archaeologist.

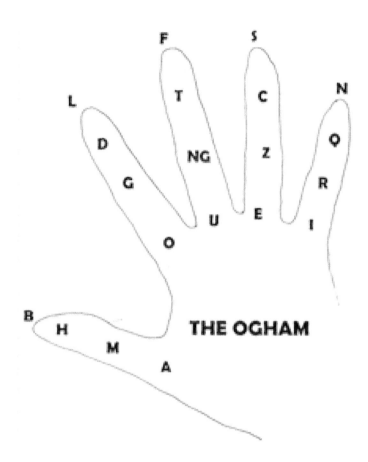

This hand signal theory fits with the original Ogham dividing neatly into four groups of five letters, which could be transferred to the tip and joints of the five fingers of a human hand.

THE OGHAM

This would also complement the numerical tally-mark systems used at that time which used the numbers five and twenty as a base and so would easily adapt to the Ogham.

Other Ogham using finger signs that could have been used for coded or secret messages include:

- **Cossogam**[32]: This describes a way of signing Ogham using the fingers against the leg. "*The fingers of the hand about the shinbone for the letters and to put them on the right of the shinbone for group B. To the left for group H. Athwart the shinbone for group M. Straight across for group A, viz, one finger for the first letter of the group, two for the second letter, till it would reach five for the fifth letter of whichever group it be.*"

- **Sronogam**[33]: This is the same as Foot-Ogham except the nose is used instead of the leg. "*The fingers of the hands about the nose viz, similiter to right and left, athwart, across*"

- **Basogam**[34]: manus aliam percutit lignorum. i.e. '*palm of hand variously strikes wood*'. Possibly the angle of the hand indicated the aicme while the number of strikes indicate the letter.

---

[32] Foot-Ogham
[33] Nose-Ogham
[34] Palm of Hand Ogham

THE OGHAM

Most Oghams appear to be variations on ways of writing the alphabet and may have been used to train the scholar's mind in cryptic thought processes, like using kennings in poetry.

However, some of the Ogham varieties could have been used as property or business records and a numerical system of tallying. Here is a sample of some of the different varieties of Ogham word lists which may have been used as a cipher, or as an aide memoire, or even a way to classify inventories:

- **Enogam**[35]: includes pheasant, duck, gull, hawk, snipe, night raven, wren, starling, hen, etc.

- **Dathogam**[36]: includes white, grey, red, fine-coloured, clear, terrible, black, brown, mouse-coloured etc.

- **Ogam tirda**[37]: includes axe, rope, hedge-bill, pack-saddle, cask, adze, cask, faggot, wedge, flail, etc.

- **Ogam Uisceach**[38]: rivulet for group B, one rivulet for B, five for N etc.; weir for group H; river for group M; well for group A.

- **Conogam**[39]: watch-dog for group B; greyhound for group H; herd's dog for group M; lapdog for group A

---

[35] Bird-Ogham
[36] Colour-Ogham
[37] Agricultural Ogam
[38] Water Ogham
[39] Dog Ogham

- **Bo-ogam**[40]: milch cow for group B; stripper[41] for group H; three-year-old heifer for group M; yearling heifer for group A.

- **Danogam**[42]: includes livelihood, pilotage, poetry, handicraft, notary work, trisyllabic poetry, wizardry, turning, harping, fluting, soldiering, smithwork, modelling, deer-stalking, dispensing, sovereignty, harvesting, etc.

Although many varieties of Ogham could be cited as evidence of Ogham's cryptic nature and as examples of how the alphabet was used for secret communication, never underestimate the fascination of the medieval mind with cryptic alphabets, or even with just having fun. Remember it was religious medieval monks, trapped for years at their desk studiously copying texts who meticulously included detailed images of cats cleaning their nether regions as part of their beautifully illustrated manuscripts.

And while we are on the subject of cats here's a 9th century poem about a cat, just for fun …

---

[40] Cow Ogham
[41] A "stripper" is a cow at the end of her lactation, giving little milk
[42] Art-Ogham

THE OGHAM

 ### Appendix 3: PANGUR BAN
"Pangur Bán" is an Old Irish poem[43], written around the 9th century at Reichenau Abbey[44] by an anonymous Irish monk and compares the cat's happy hunting with his own scholarly pursuits. Although the poem is anonymous, it is believed to be the work of Sedulius Scottus[45] as it is similar to other poetry that he wrote.

Pangur, white Pangur, How happy we are
Alone together, scholar and cat

Each has his own work to do daily;
For you it is hunting, for me study.

Your shining eye watches the wall;
My feeble eye is fixed on a book.

You rejoice, when your claws entrap a mouse;
I rejoice when my mind fathoms a problem.

Pleased with his own art, neither hinders the other;
Thus we live ever without tedium and envy.

---

[43] The poem is preserved in the Reichenau Primer and is now kept in St. Paul's Abbey
[44] The Benedictine abbey on the island of Reichenau was a centre of scholarship, where Irish monks created some of the finest illuminated manuscripts ever produced
[45] Sedulius Scottus was an Irish teacher, Latin grammarian and scriptural commentator who lived in the 9th century

THE OGHAM

Thank you to Linda Godden for her illustrations and her encouragement, Pat Ritter my big-hearted mentor from the Pomona Writers Group for his hands-on help, and to my husband Roy who listens and gives a truthful reaction.

This book is offered for your interest. Please be aware that this is general information only so if you seek cures, it is wiser not to self-medicate but instead see your doctor, herbalist or naturopath. Although tree medicine is natural it is certainly not harmless and should be approached with prudent respect and cautious awe.

Sue Bagust
ideas@westnet.com.au

Printed in Great Britain
by Amazon

12899228R00062